Baseball Is Fun!

by Robin Nelson

first step nonfiction

Lerner Publications Company · Minneapolis

LERNER

SOURCE

Expand learning beyond the printed book. Download free, complementary educational resources for this book from our website, www.lerneresource.com.

The images in this book are used with the permission of: © iStockphoto.com/reanas, p. 4; © iStockphoto.com/ Justin Horrocks, p. 5; © Erik Isakson/Getty Images, p. 6; © iStockphoto.com/kali9, pp. 7, 9; © Kelpfish/ Dreamstime.com, p. 8; © iStockphoto.com/Rob Friedman, pp. 10, 11, 12, 13; © Eye Ubiquitous/SuperStock, p. 14; © Donato16/Dreamstime.com, p. 15; © Susan Leggett/Dreamstime.com, p. 16; © iStockphoto.com/ YinYang, p. 17; © Photographerlondon/Dreamstime.com, p. 18; © iStockphoto.com/Loretta Hostettler, p. 19.

Front Cover: © Stockagogo, Craig Barhorst/Shutterstock.com.

Main body text set in ITC Avant Garde Gothic Std Medium 21/25.
Typeface provided by Adobe Systems.

Lerner Publications Company
A division of Lerner Publishing Group, Inc.
241 First Avenue North
Minneapolis, MN 55401 U.S.A.

Website address: www.lernerbooks.com

Library of Congress Cataloging-in-Publication Data

Nelson, Robin, 1971–
    Baseball is fun! / by Robin Nelson.
        p.   cm. — (First step nonfiction—Sports are fun!)
    Includes index.
    ISBN 978–1–4677–1101–2 (lib. bdg. : alk. paper)
    ISBN 978–1–4677–1743–4 (eBook)
    1. Baseball—Juvenile literature. I. Title.
GV867.5.N456 2014
796.357—dc23   2012033862

Manufactured in the United States of America
1 – PC – 7/15/13

Table of Contents

Do you like to throw or hit a ball?

You can play baseball!

Two teams play baseball.

The team that scores the
most **runs** wins.

You need a ball, a bat, and a **glove** to play baseball.

8

Batters wear **helmets** to protect their heads.

Batter Up!

The **pitcher** throws the ball.

The batter hits the ball.

The batter runs to first **base**.

The other team tries to get
the ball to first base.

The ball gets to first base before the batter gets there.

The batter is **out**.

Another batter hits the ball.

She gets to first base
before the ball. She is safe!

The batter runs to second base when her team gets another hit.

They get still another hit. The batter races to third. She makes it to **home plate**!

When she gets to home plate, her team gets a run.

The Baseball Field

A baseball field has four bases, including home plate. Sometimes a baseball field is called a baseball diamond. Can you guess why?